Flowers series 9
Bubbly Picture Books

Copyright
Flowers series 9
Bubbly Picture Books
Edition 1-2020

All rights reserved.
Copyright with the Author and Photographer: Dr. Harpal Sodhi

Preface

"Flowers Series 9, Bubbly Picture Books, Edition 1- 2020,"
Bubbly Picture books, of Flowers Series, exhibit beautiful photographs of unique flowers. This book has a variety of adorable flowers. The topic though age old, it serves as a common subject matter for artists, educators, printers and businessmen.

The beautiful photographs of flowers are in fact for multipurpose. This book has around 26 pages and is published as e-book and paperback edition. There are numerous flowers Series that have been published. The photography is from USA.

Bubbly Picture Books on different other subjects are in the process of being published as e-books and paper-back edition 1- 2020.
Author and Photographer: Dr. Harpal Sodhi.

DR. HARPAL SODHI

Contents
Title
Copyright
Preface
Content
Flowers page 5 to page 26

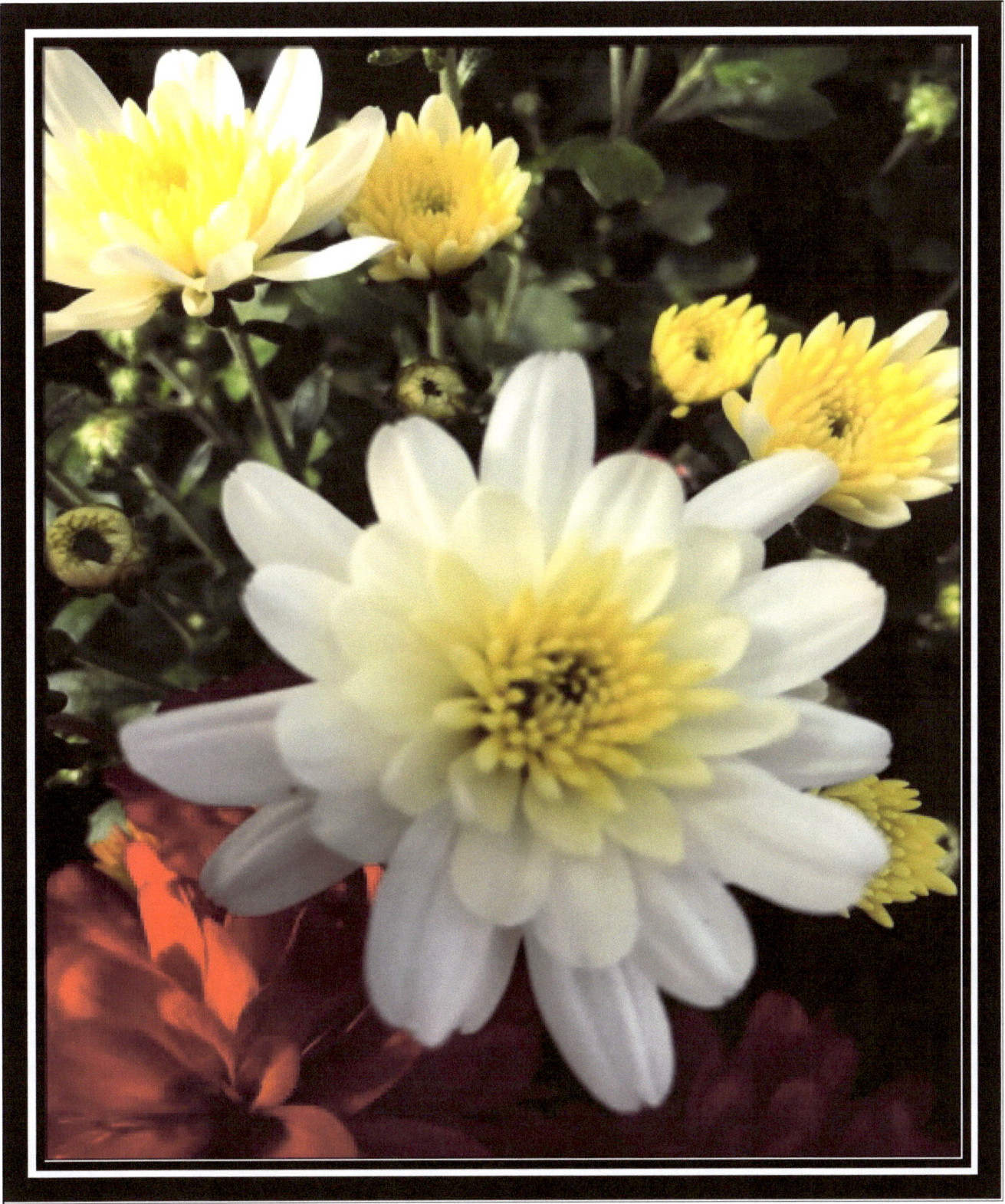

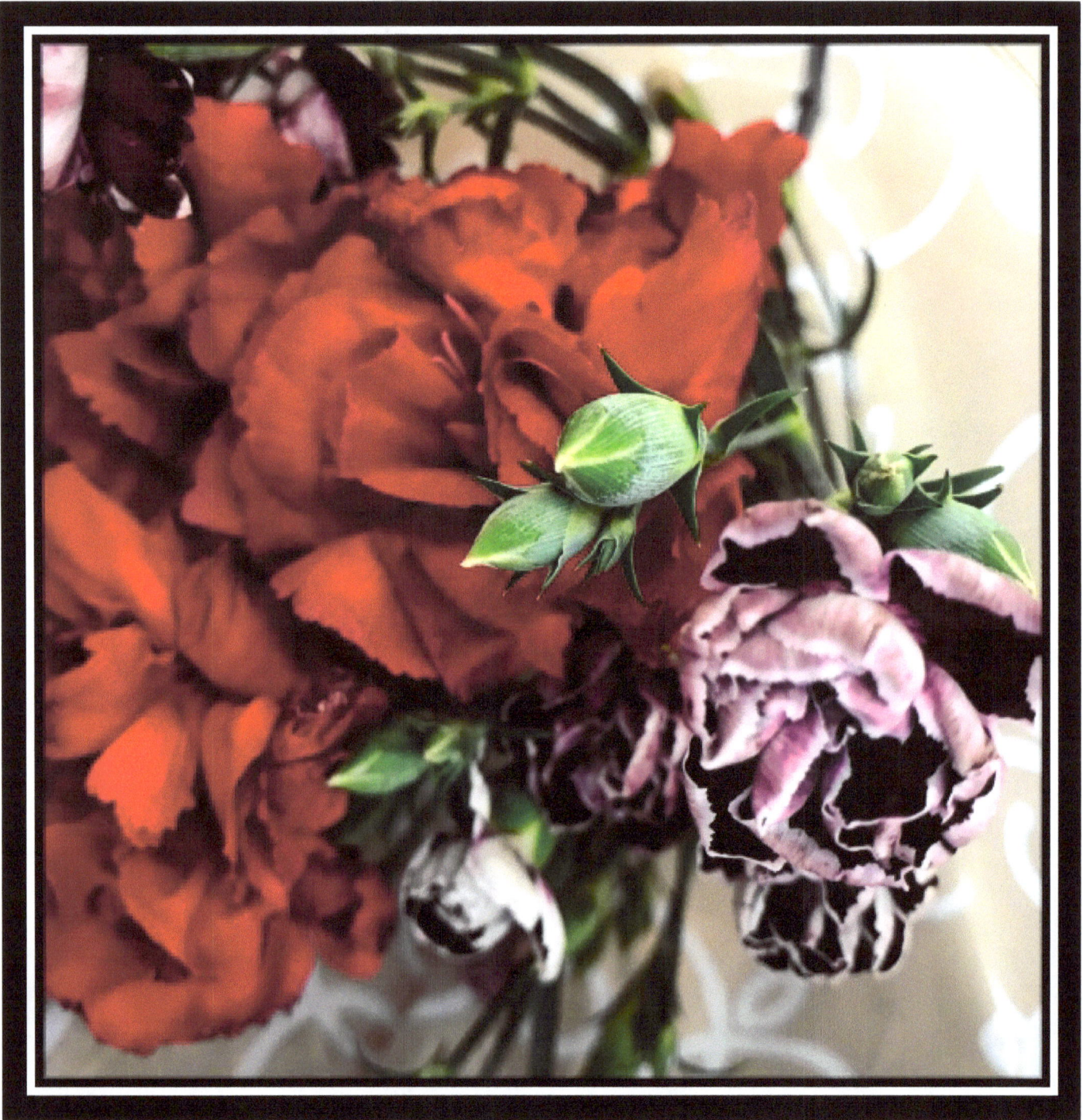

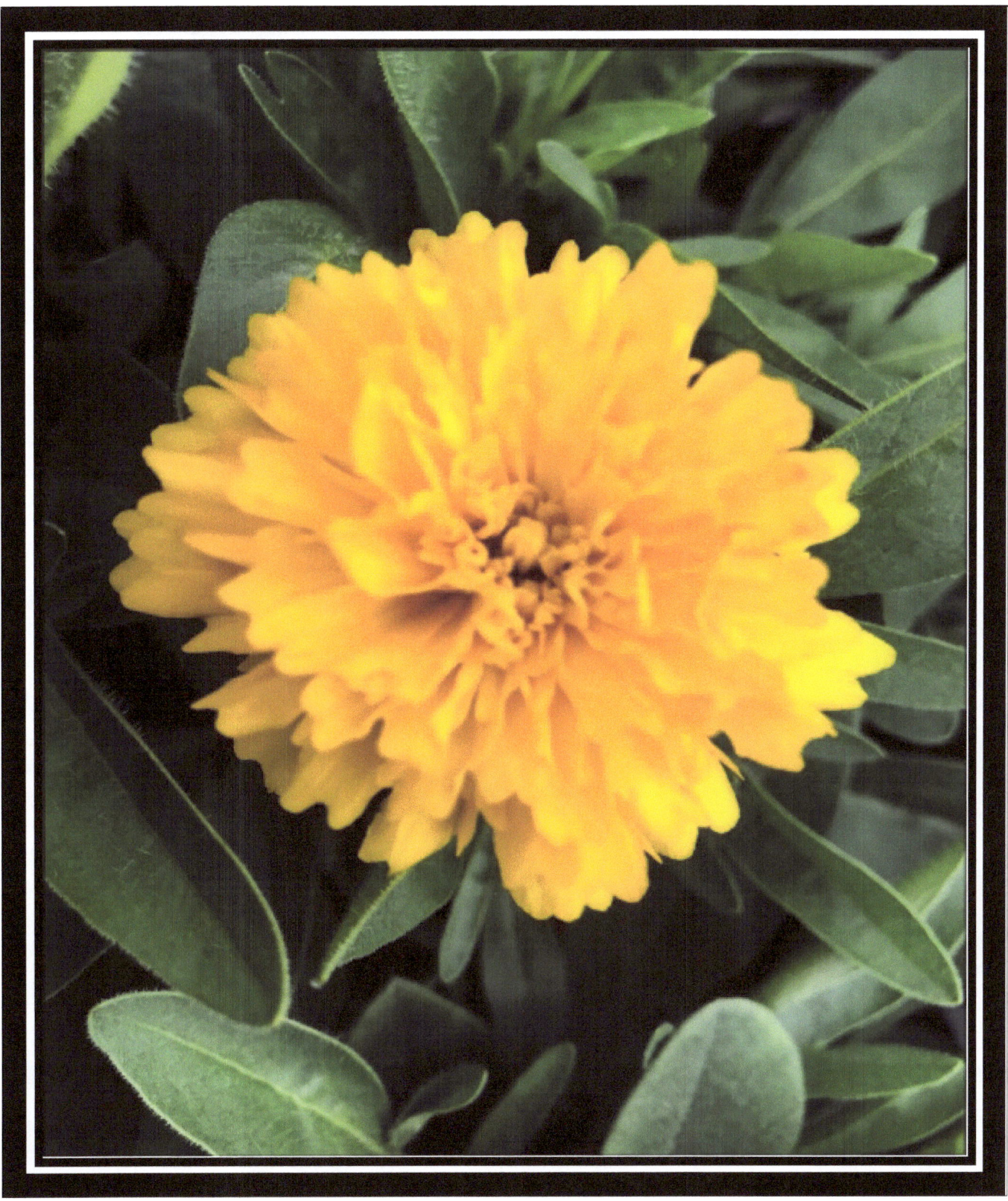

DR. HARPAL SODHI

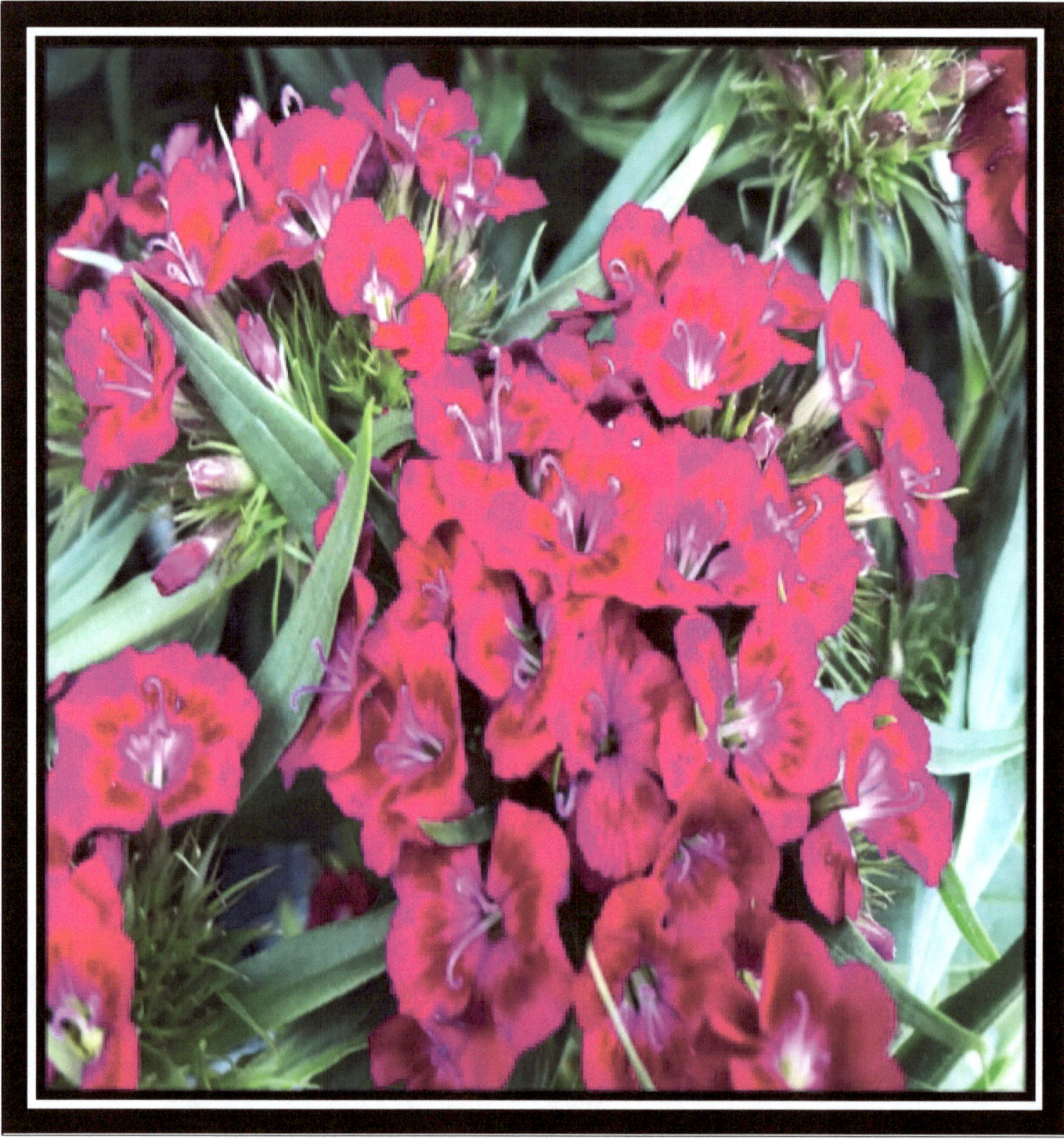

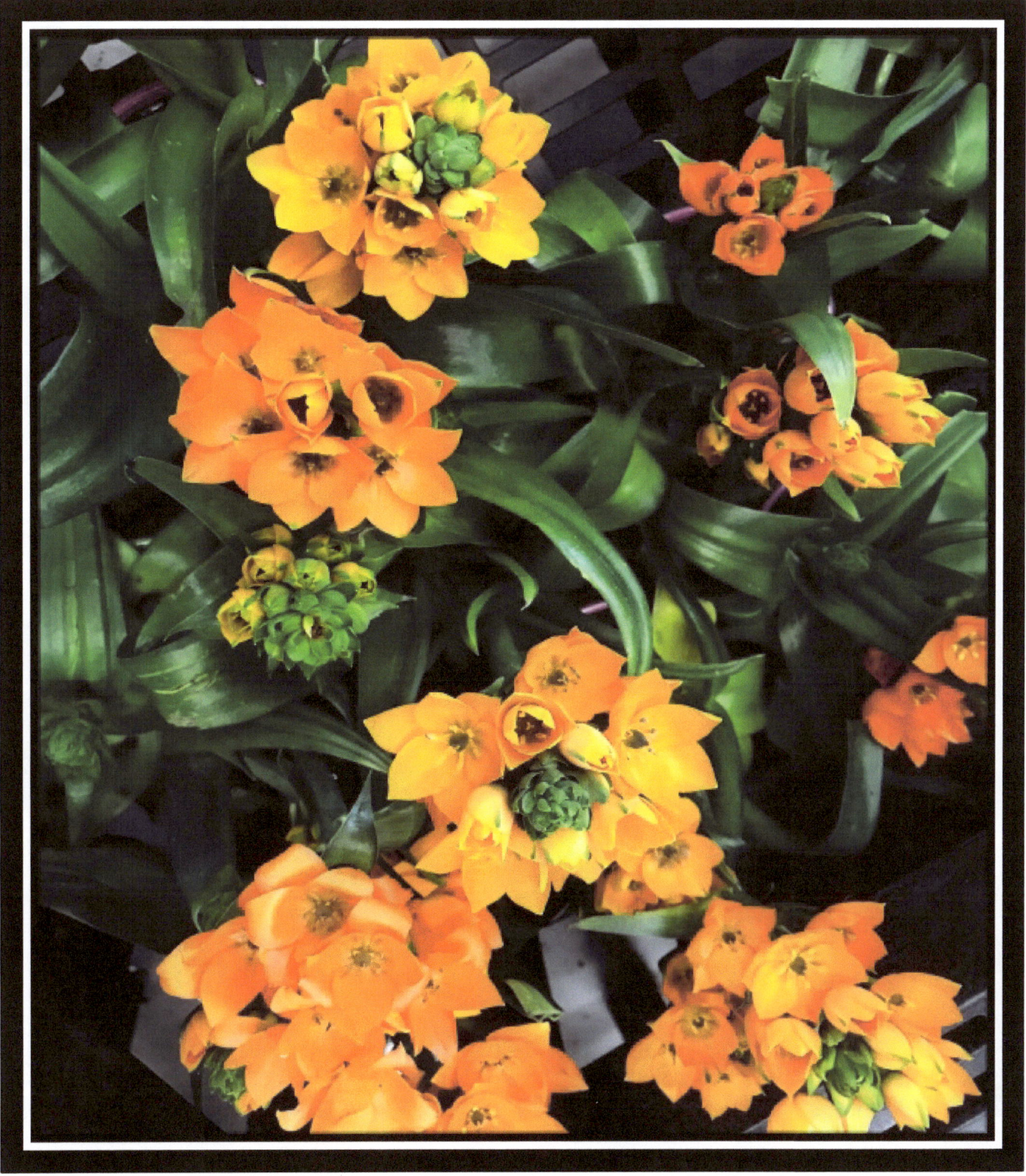

DR. HARPAL SODHI

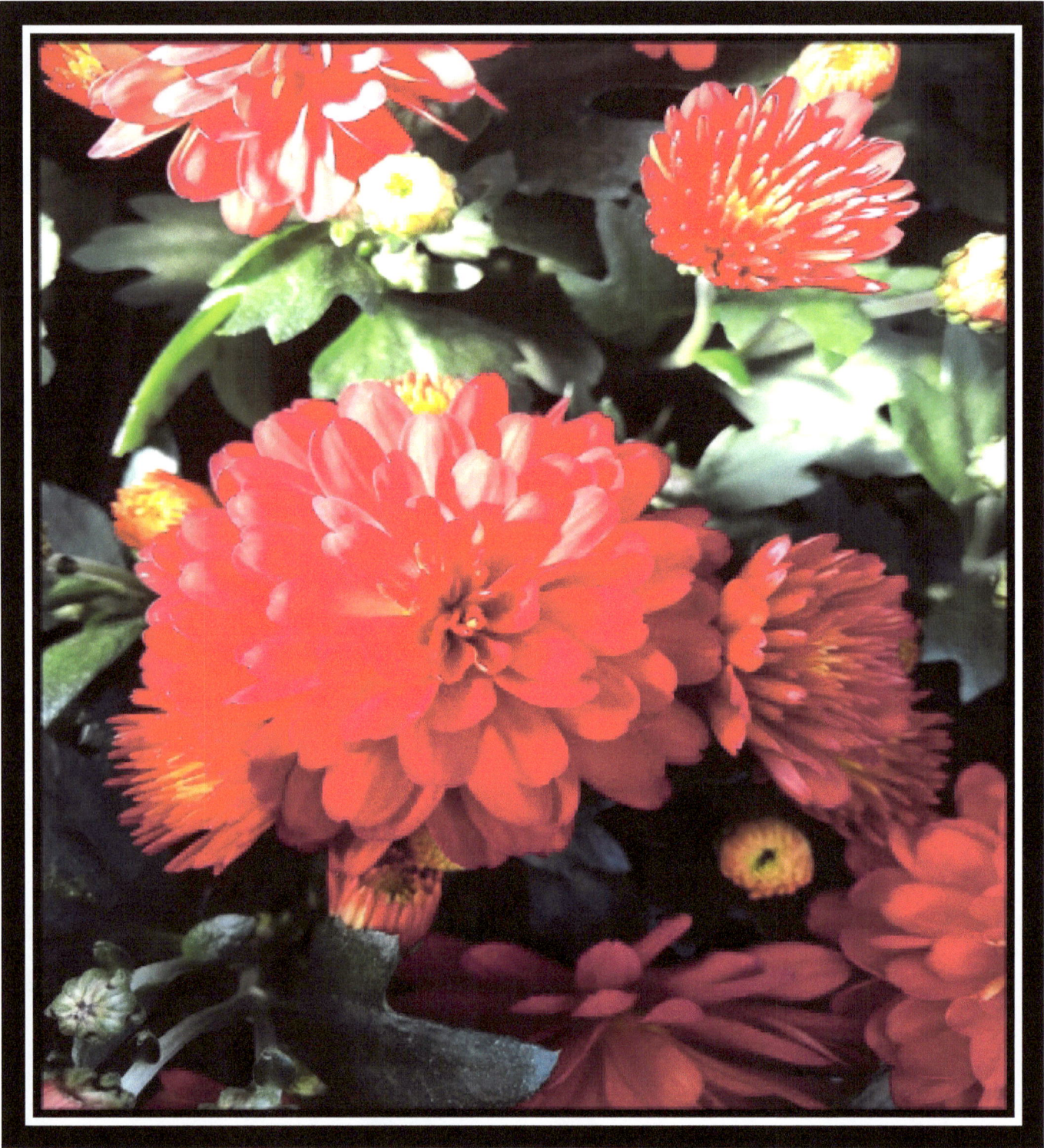

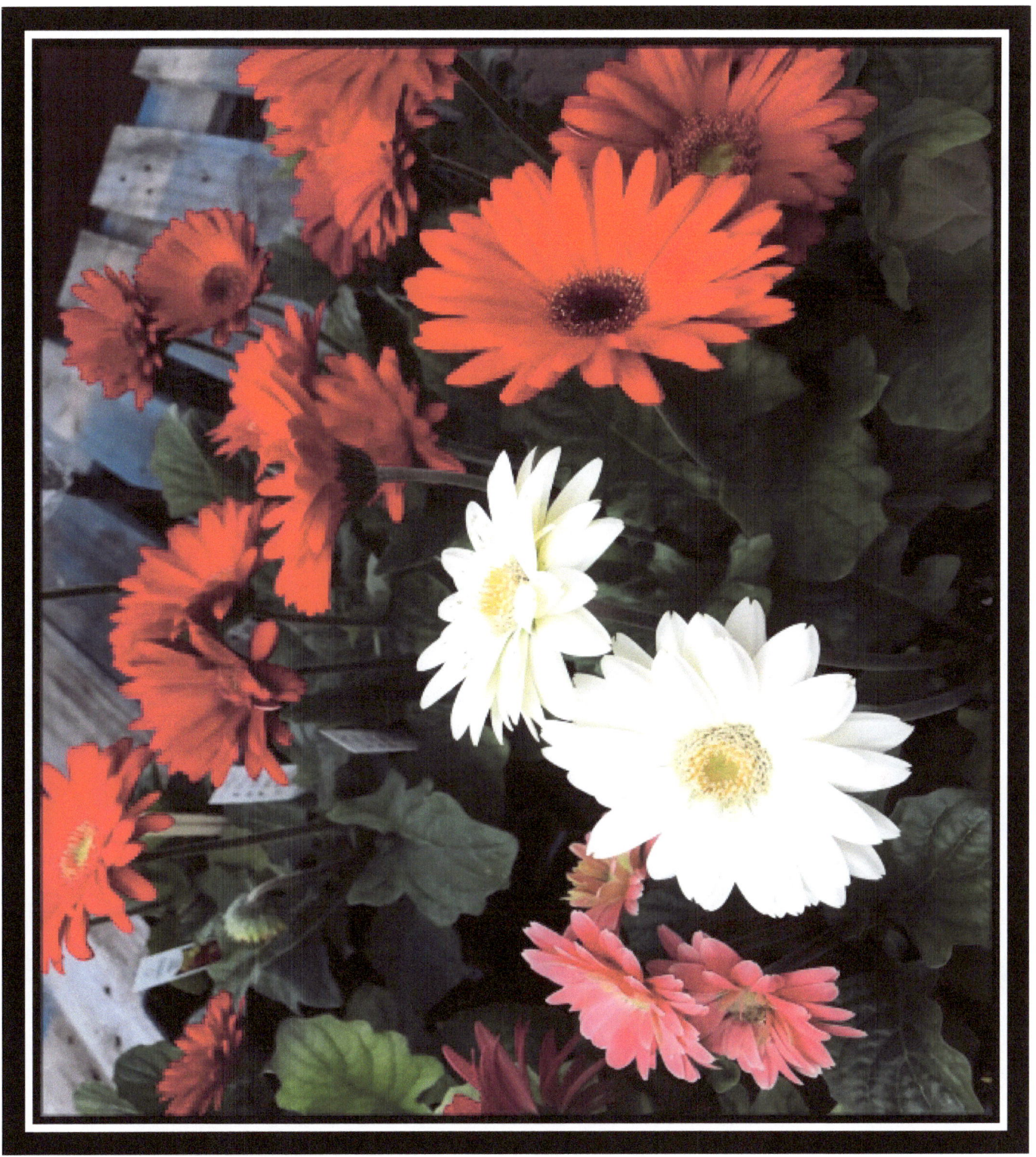

DR. HARPAL SODHI

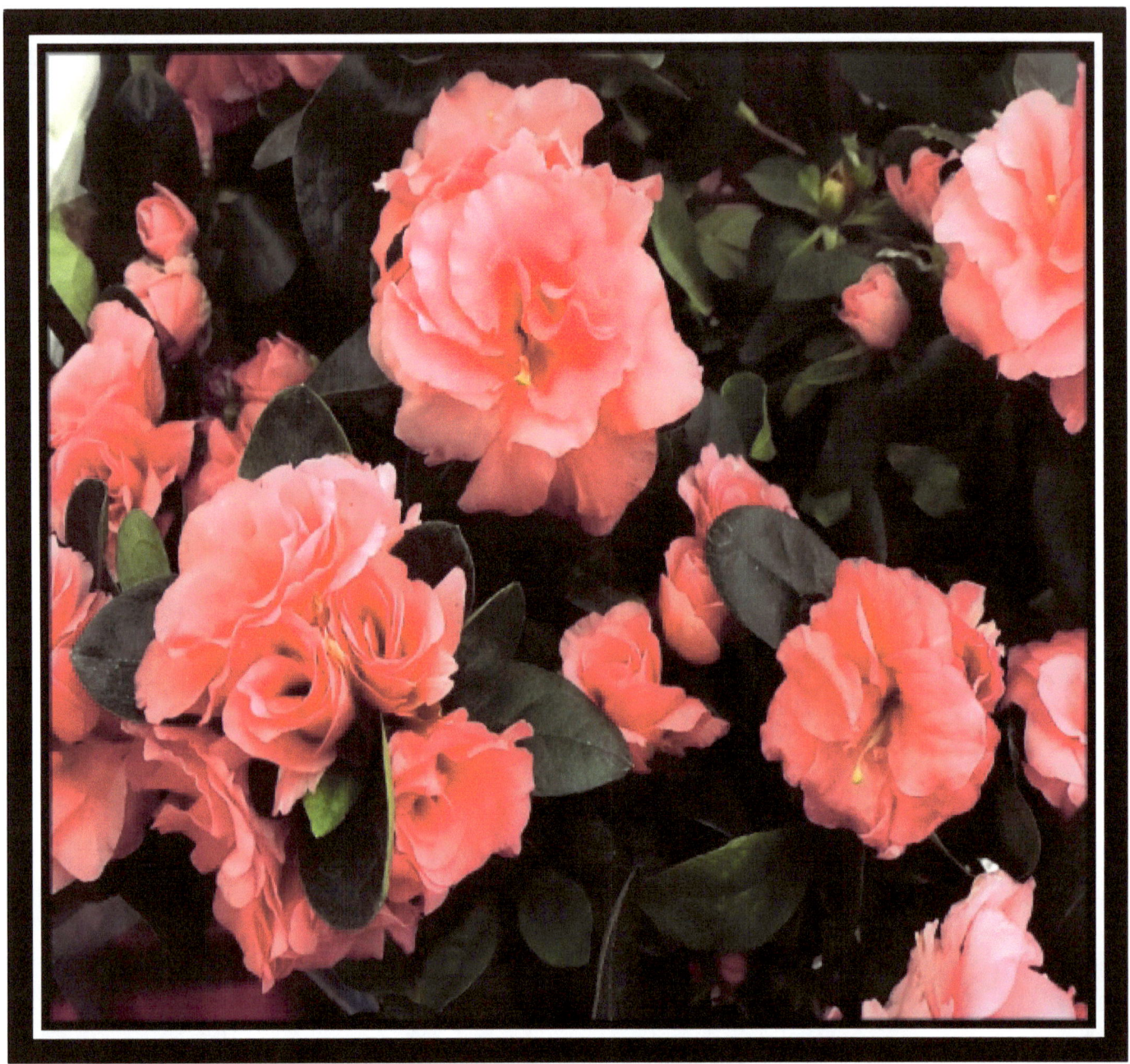

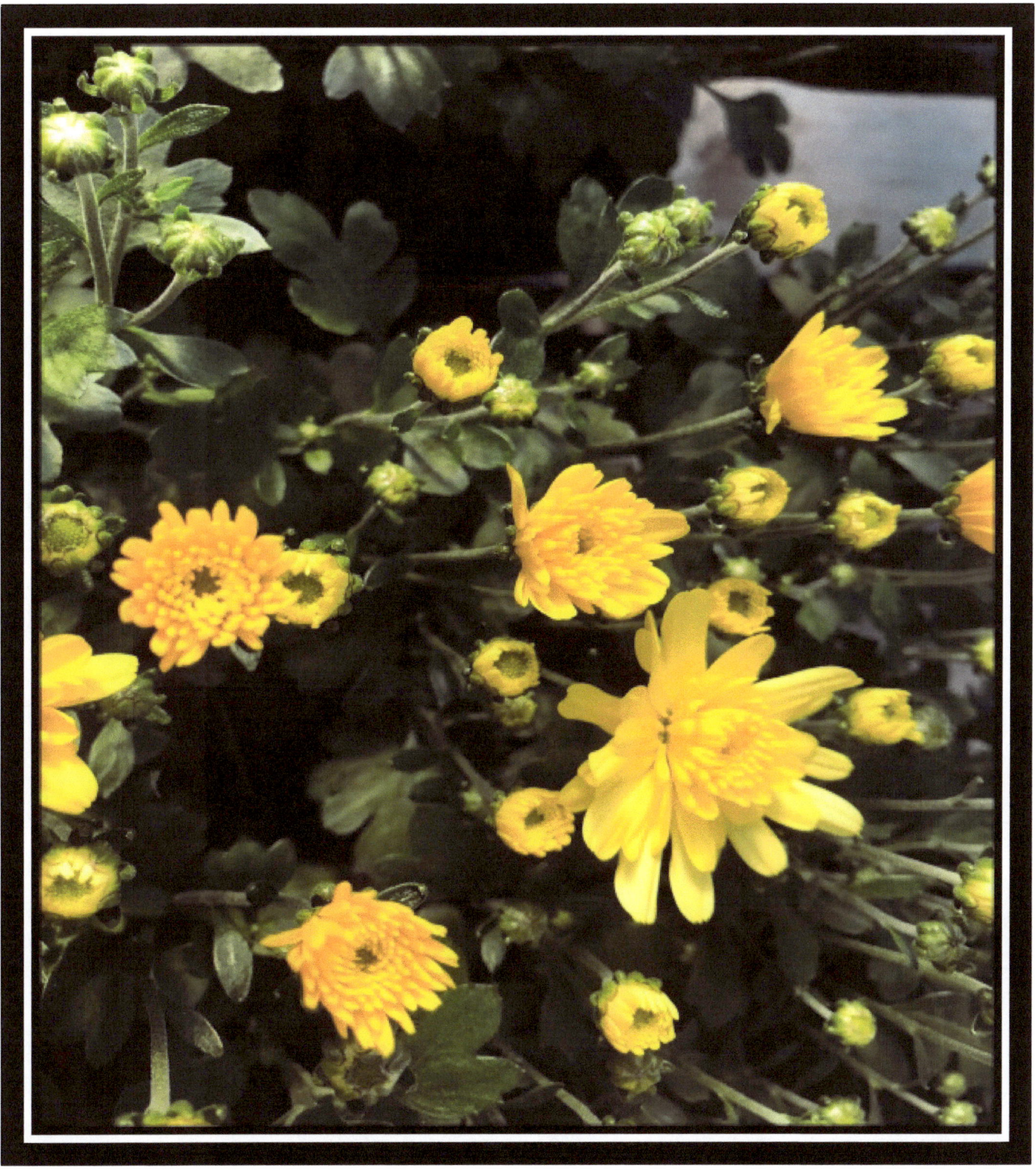

DR. HARPAL SODHI

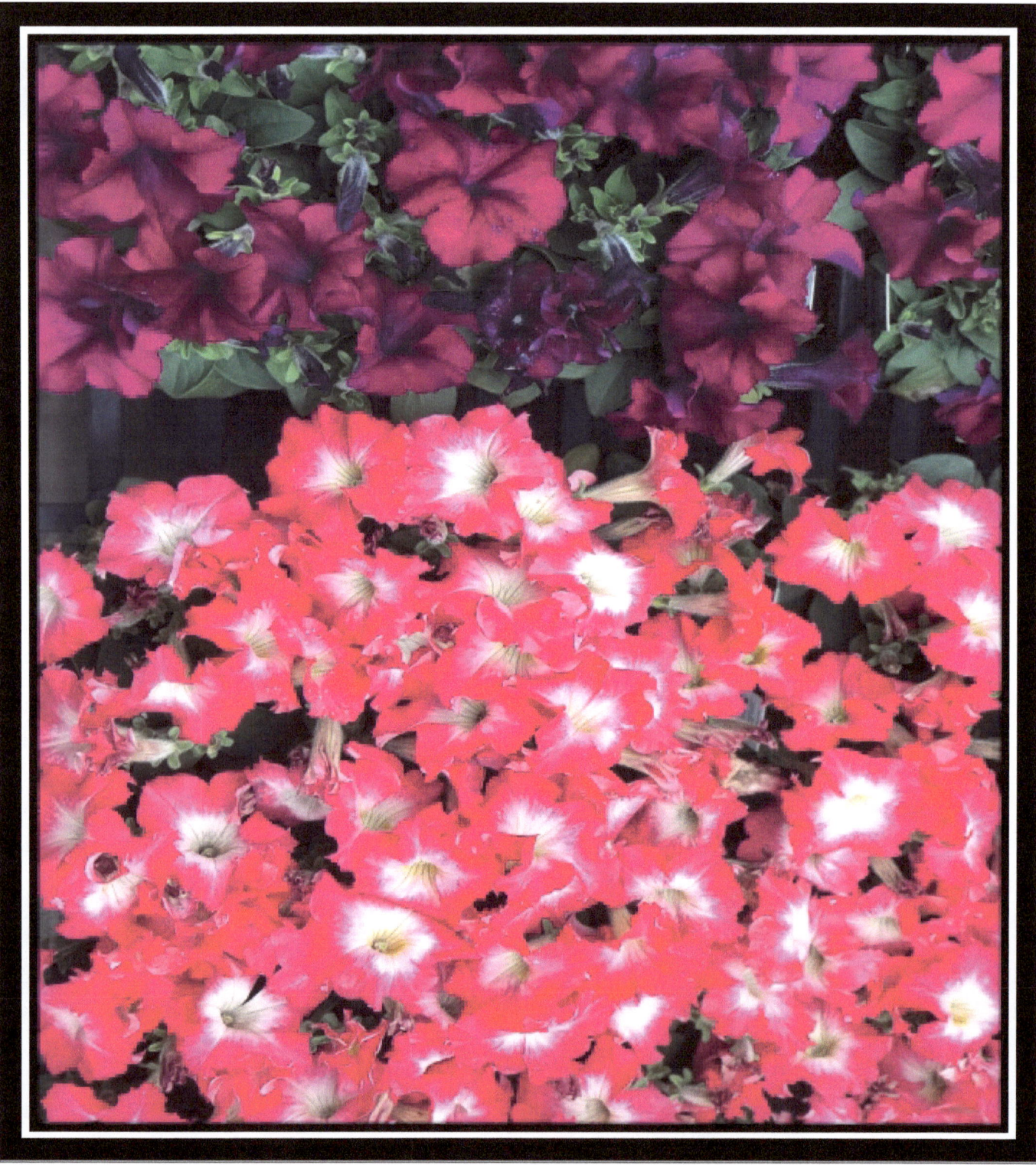

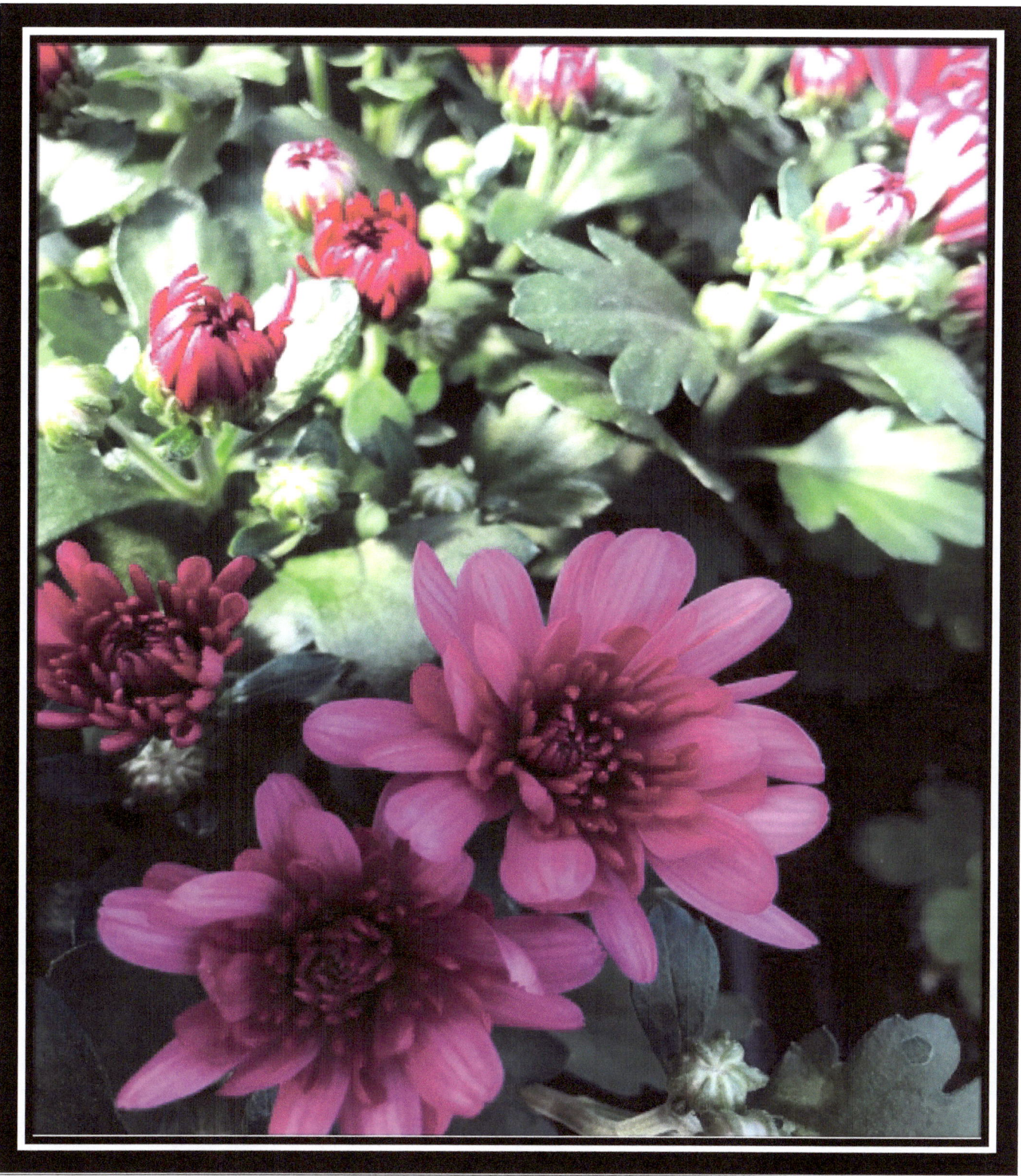

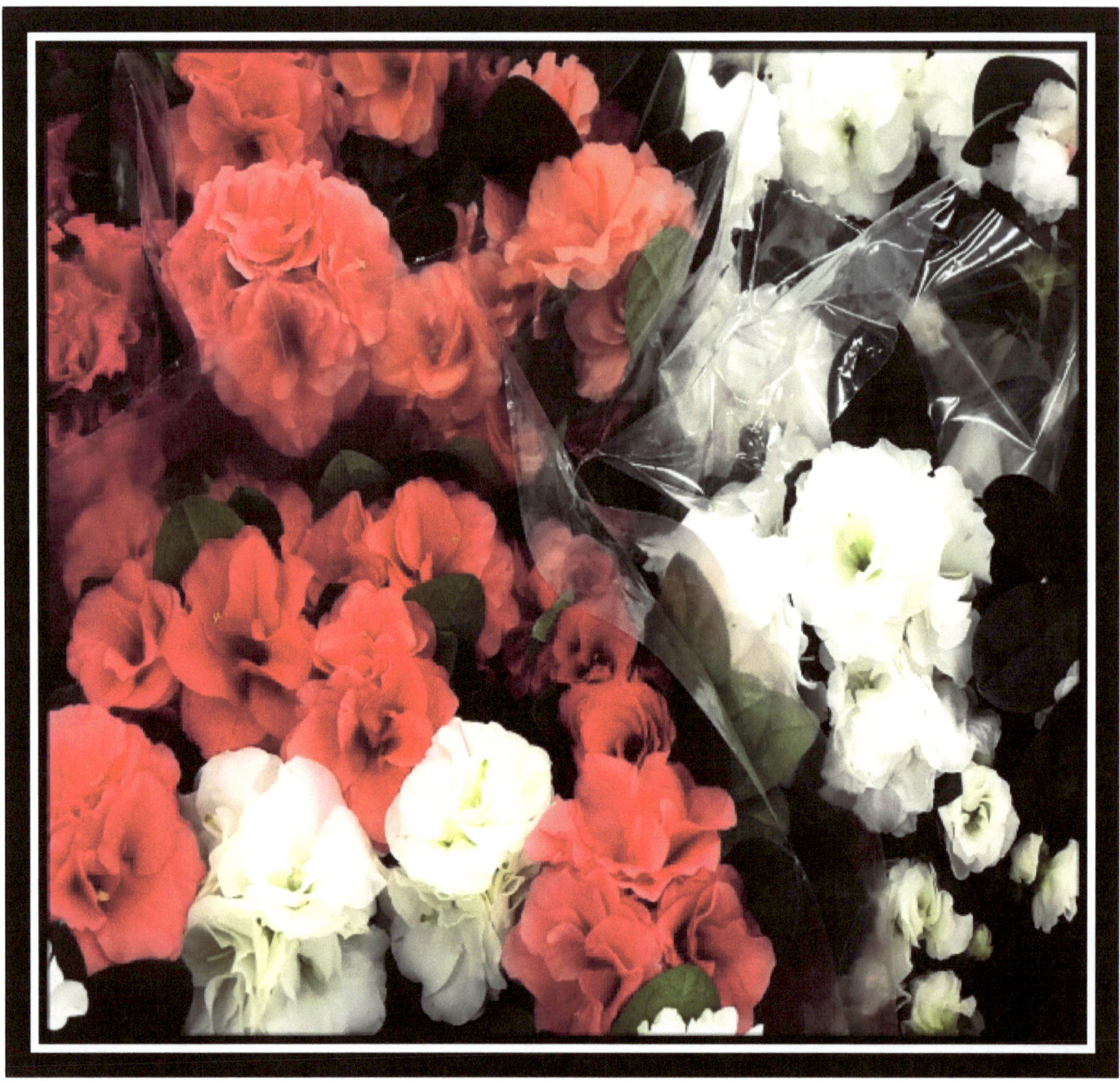

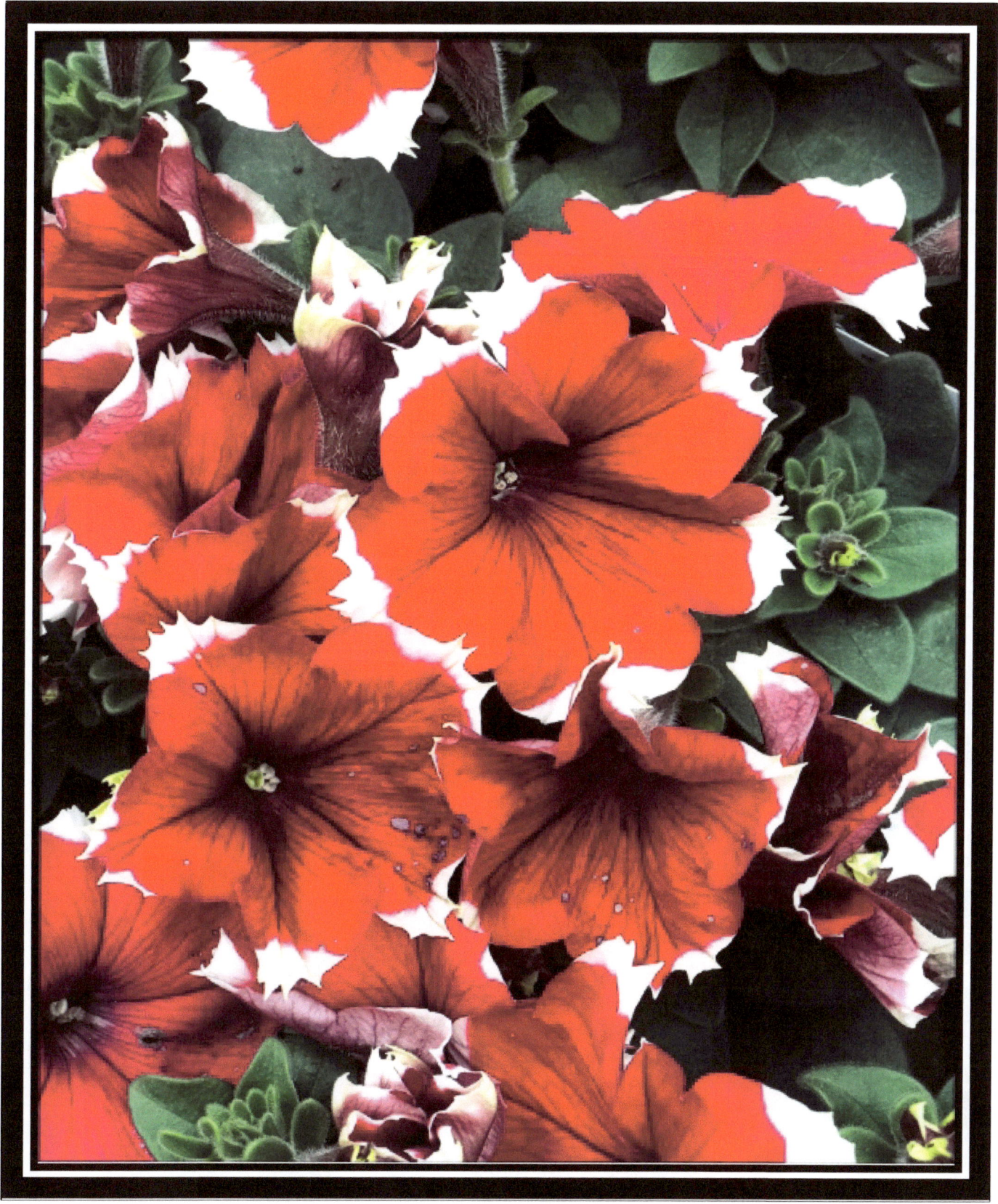

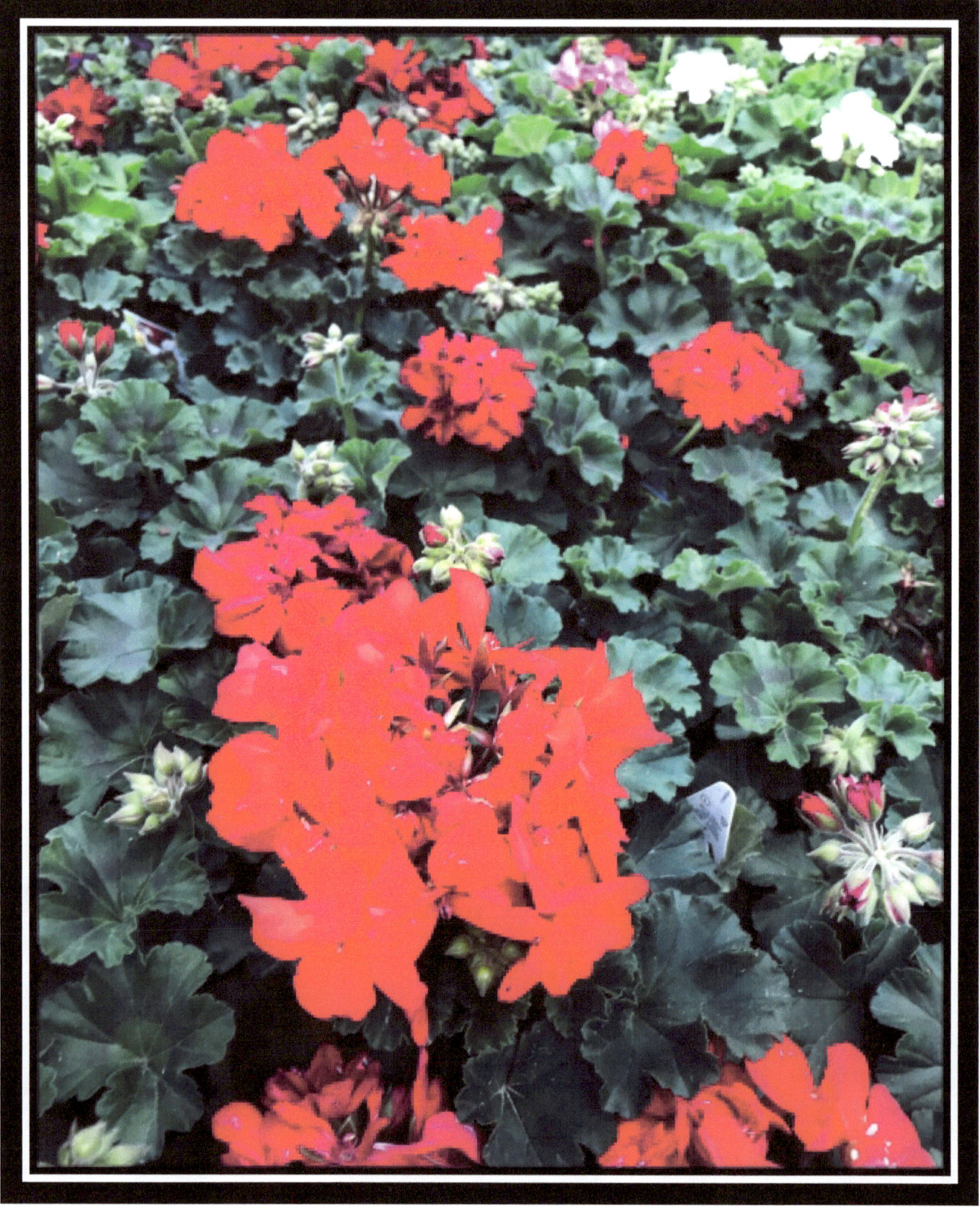

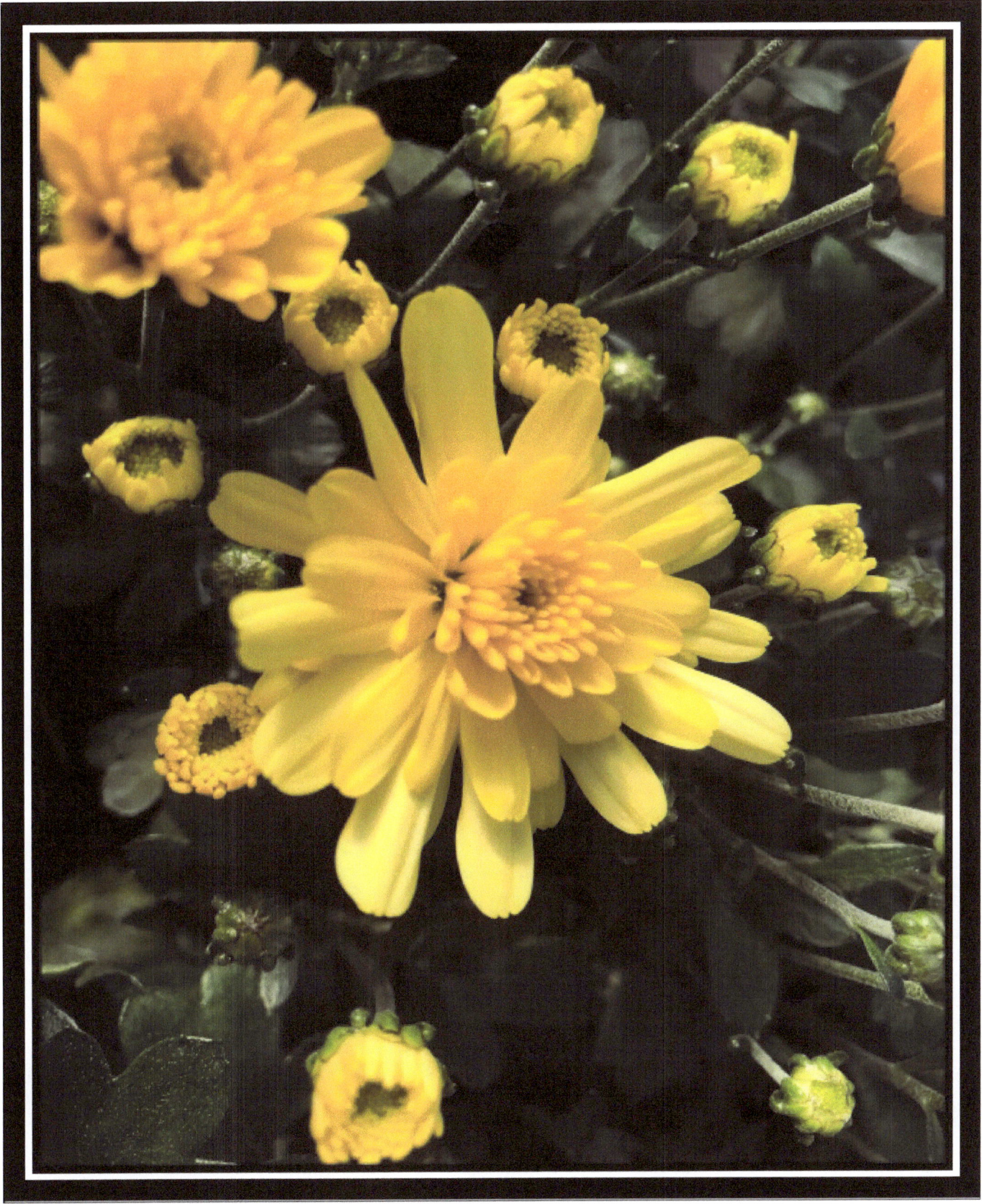

DR. HARPAL SODHI

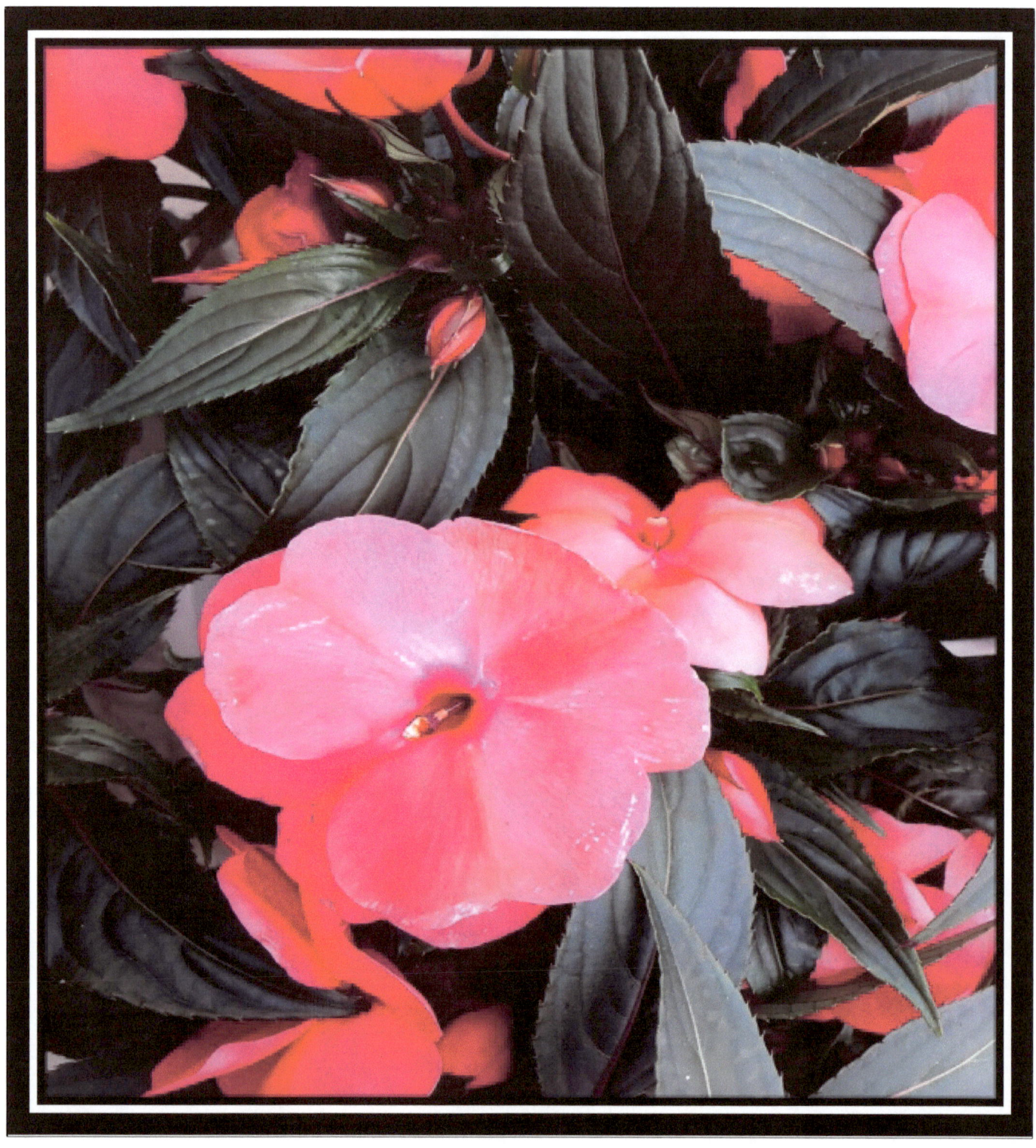

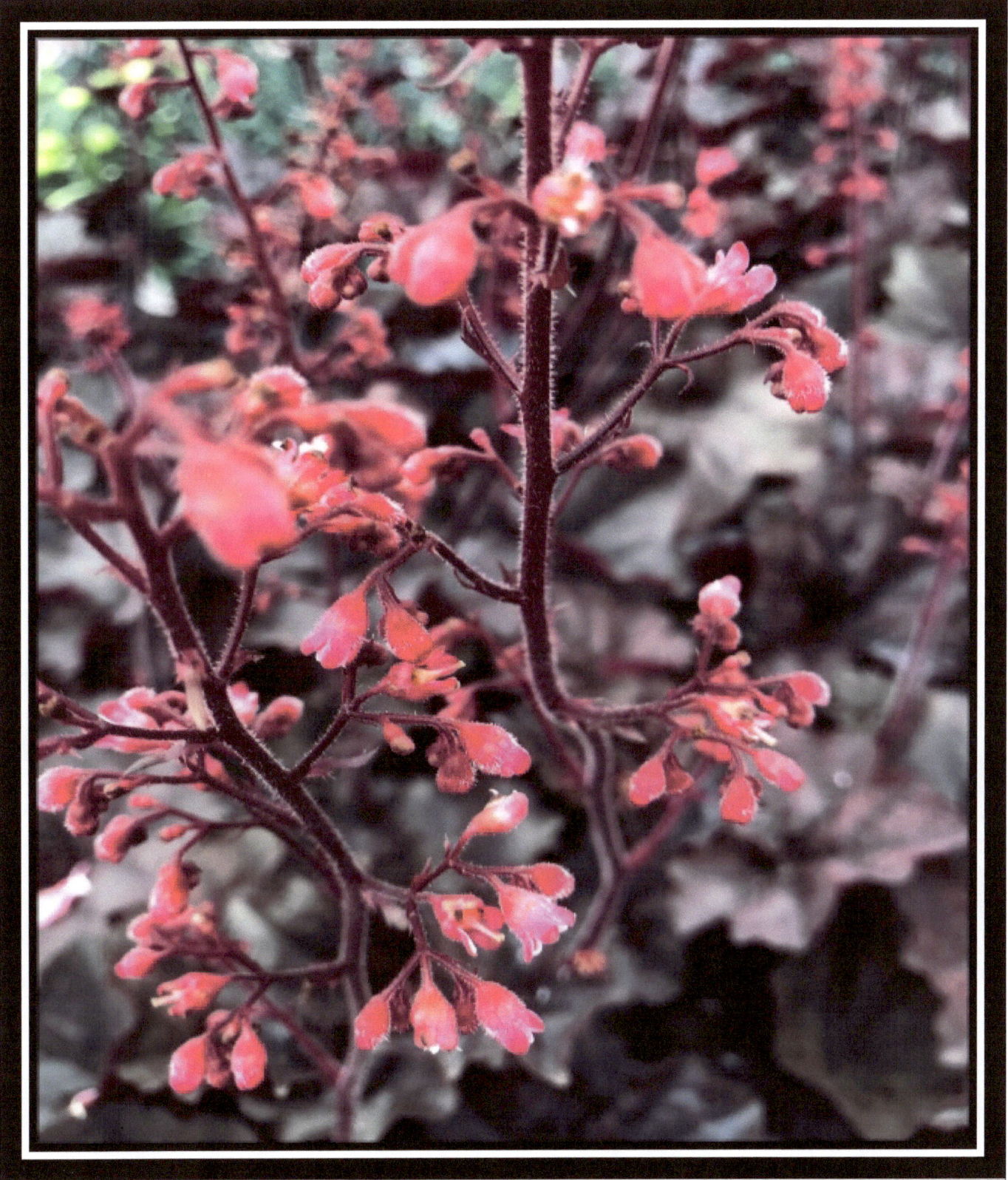

DR. HARPAL SODHI

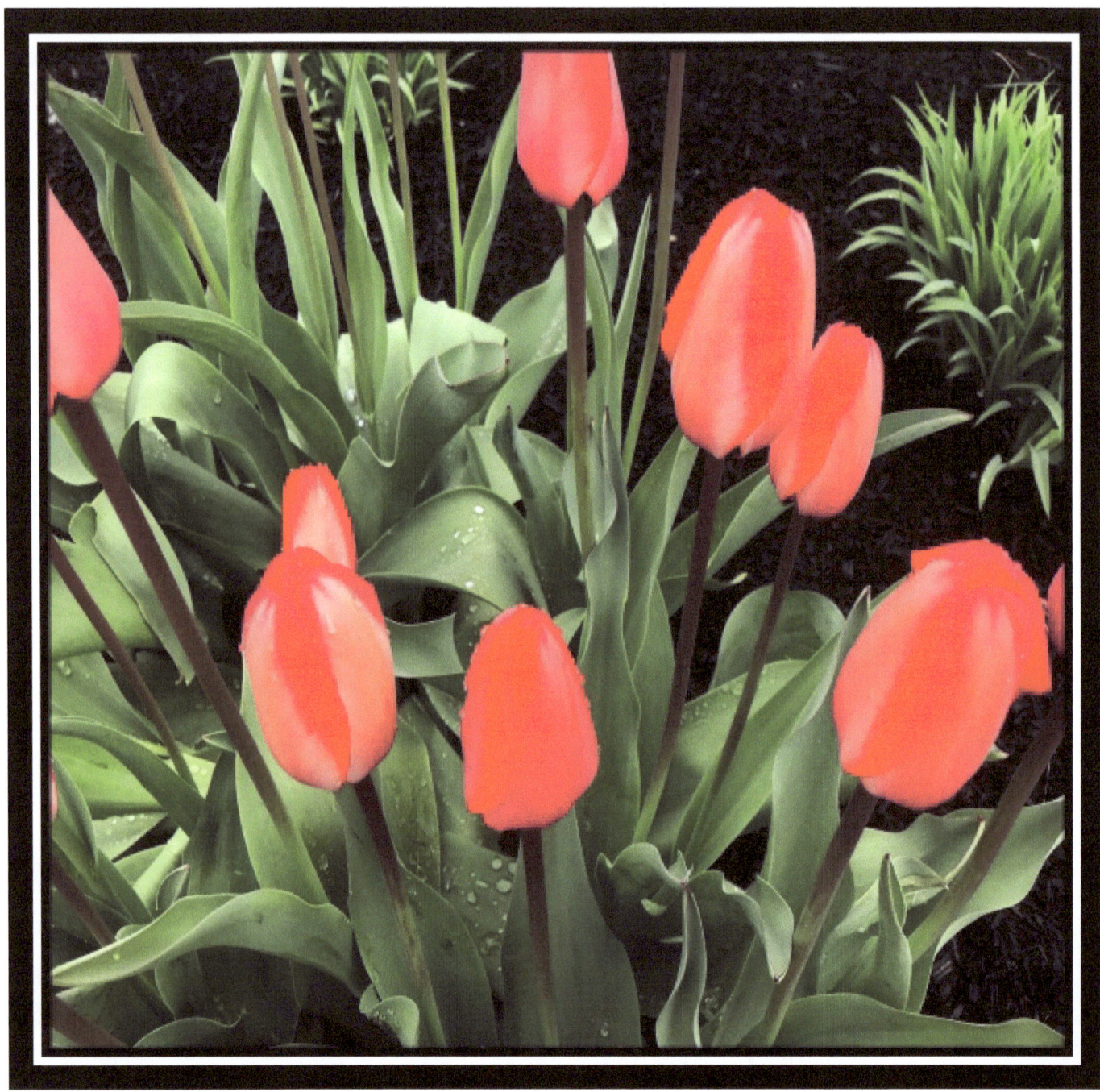

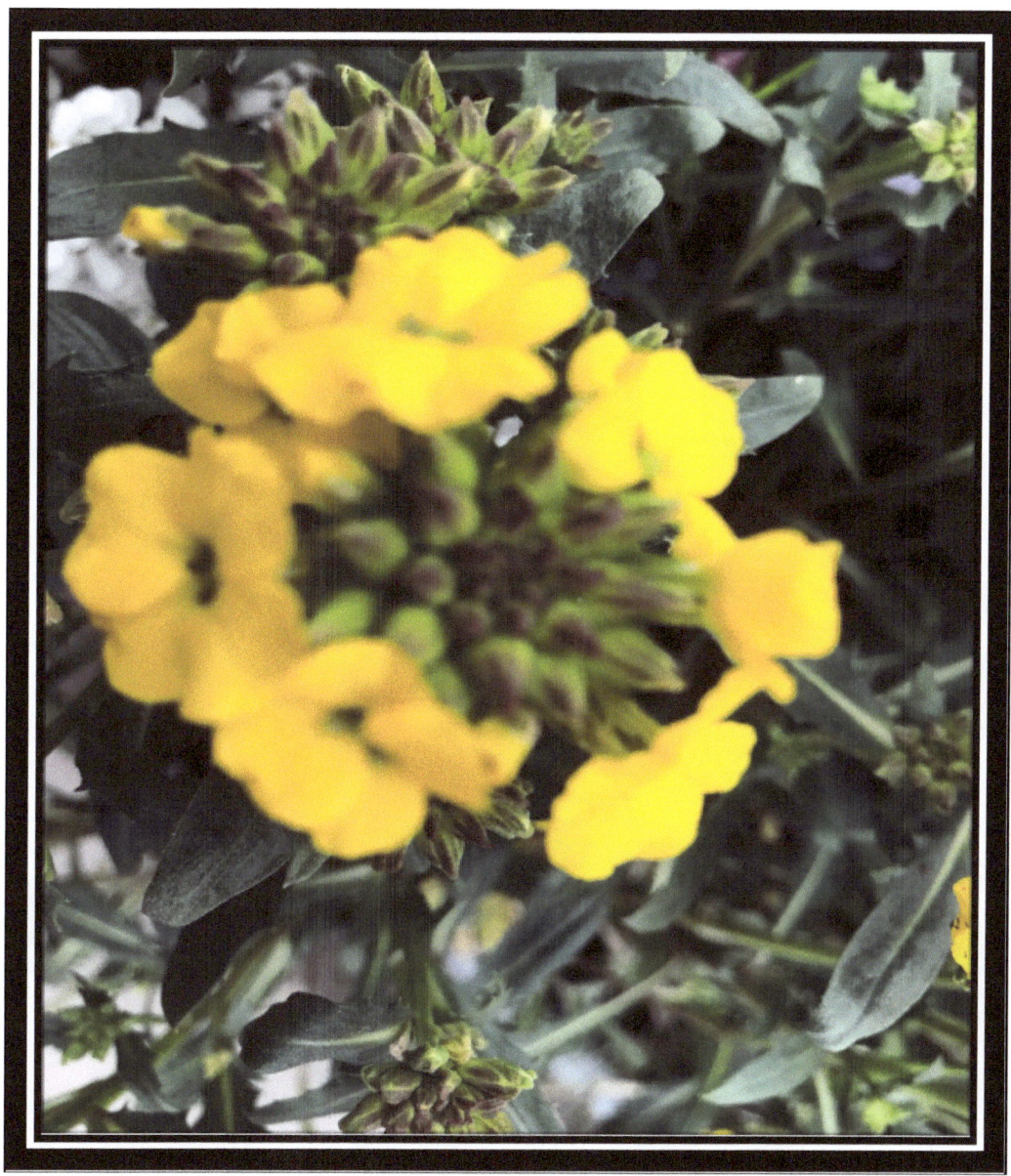

DR. HARPAL SODHI

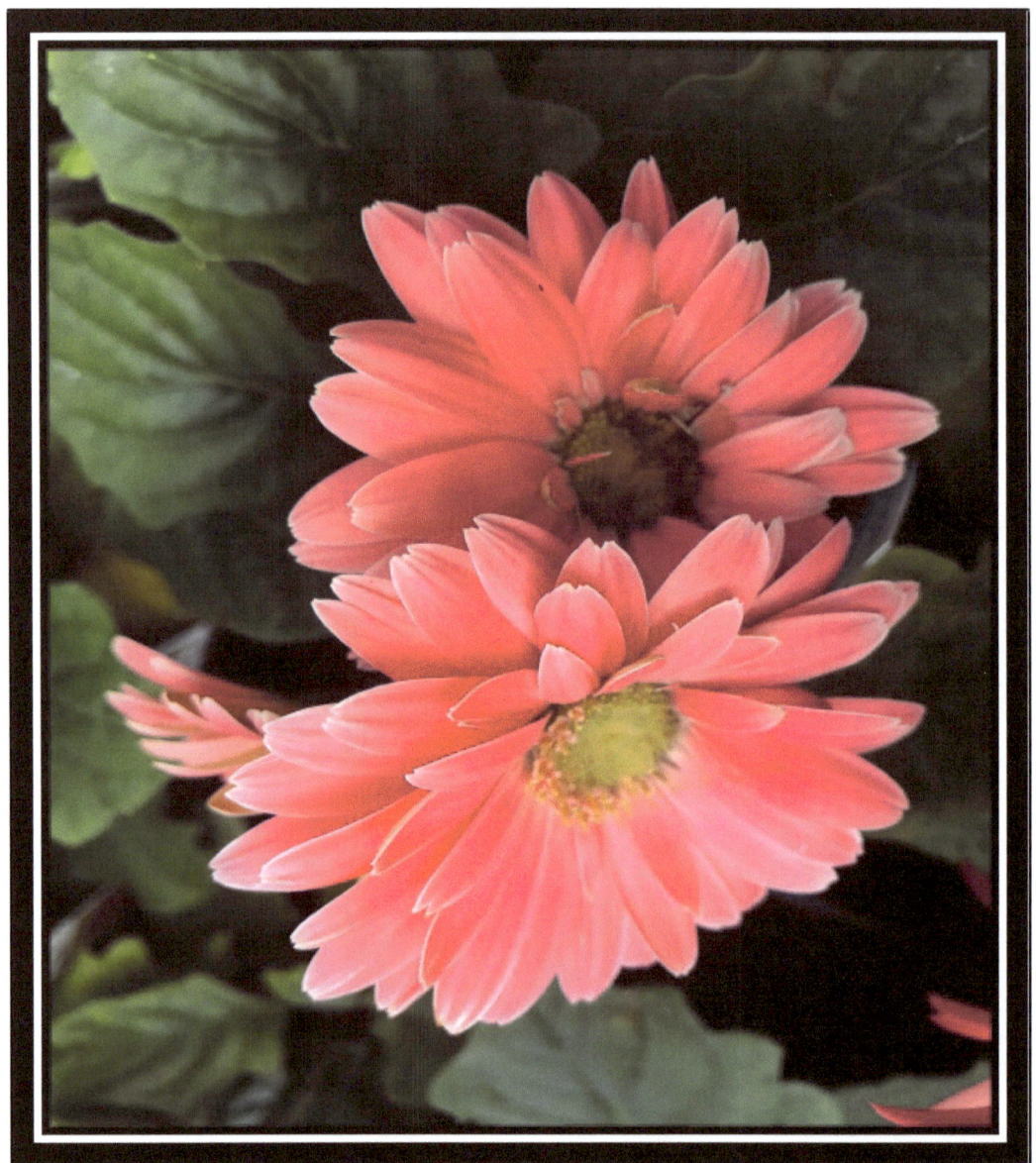

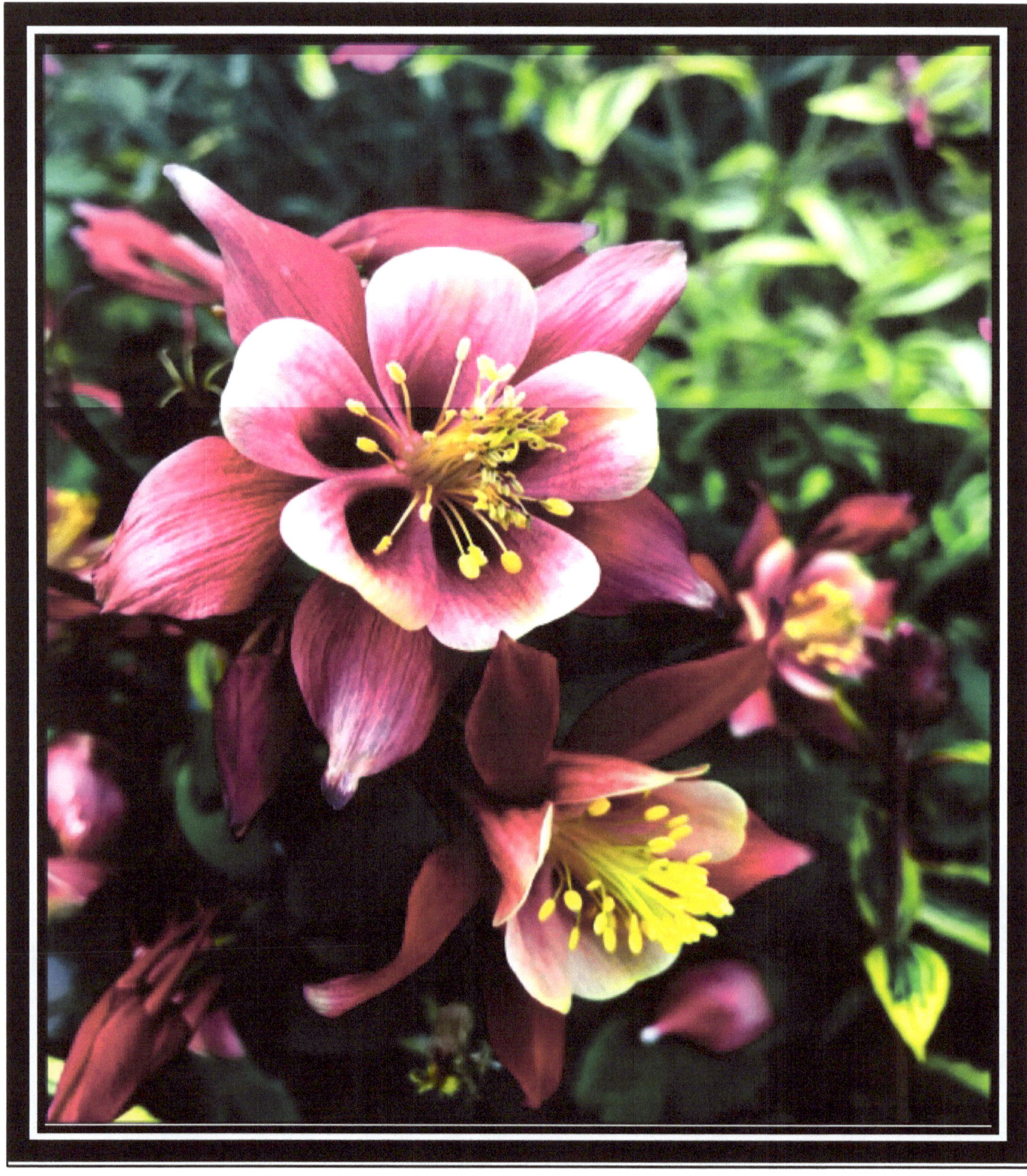

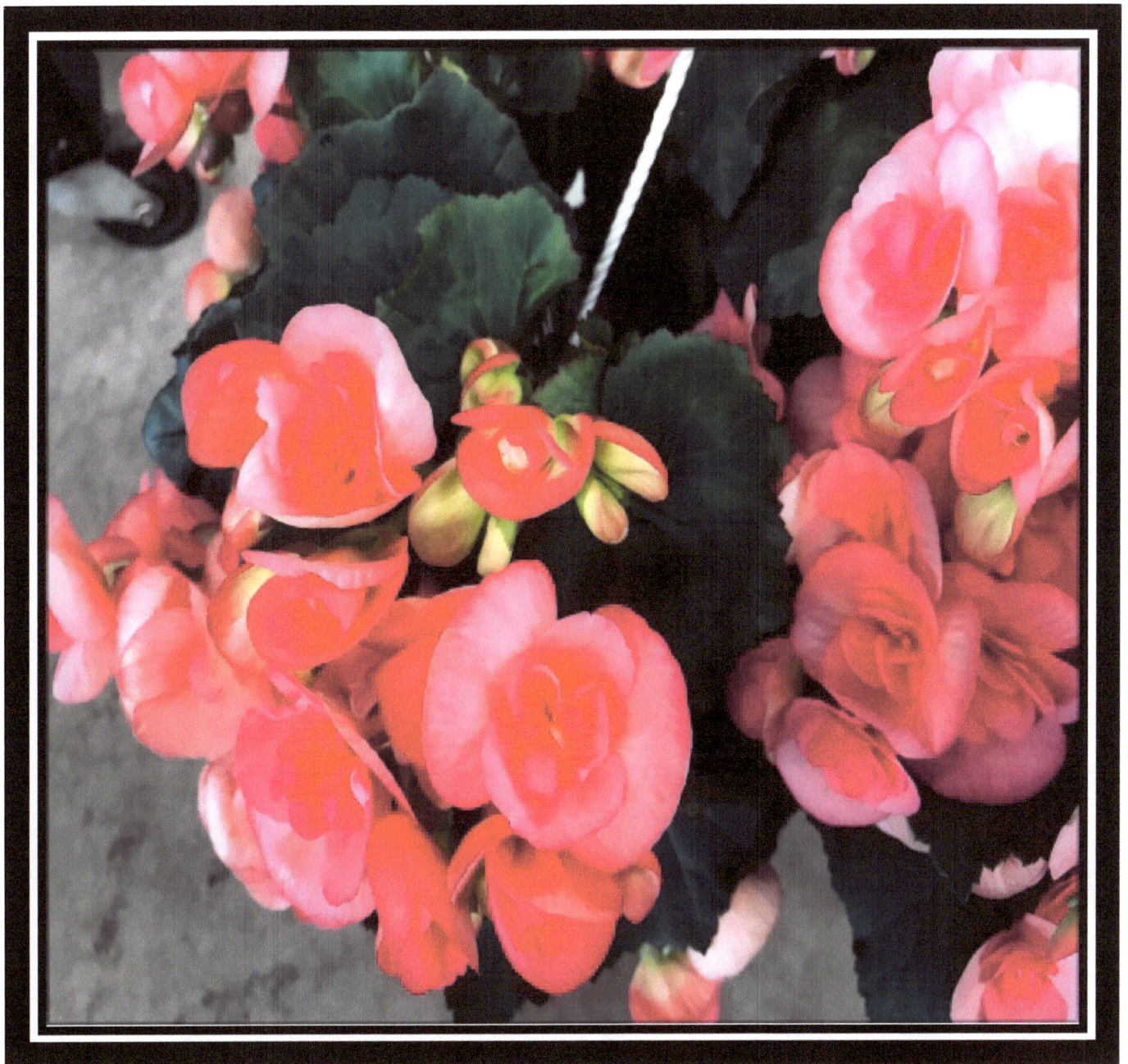

www.ingramcontent.com/pod-product-compliance
Lightning Source LLC
Chambersburg PA
CBHW051833210526
45473CB00005B/1856